Sally Derby • *Illustrated by* Mika Song

A New School Year

Stories in Six Voices

ini Charlesbridge

With love to my daughters-in-law: Lisa, Suzie, Nicki, Daphne, Marjie, and Nicole. If the choice had been mine, I would have picked you.—S. D.

To Grandpa Harry.—M. S.

Published by Charlesbridge
85 Main Street
Watertown, MA 02472
(617) 926-0329
www.charlesbridge.com

Library of Congress Cataloging-in-Publication Data
Names: Derby, Sally, author. | Song, Mika, illustrator.
Title: A new school year: poem stories in six voices/Sally Derby; illustrated by Mika Song.
Description: Watertown, MA: Charlesbridge, 2017.
Identifiers: LCCN 2016009216 (print) | LCCN 2016021095 (ebook) |
ISBN 9781580897303 (reinforced for library use) | ISBN 9781607349754 (ebook) |
ISBN 9781607349761 (ebook pdf)
Subjects: | CYAC: Schools—Juvenile poetry.
Classification: LCC PS3554.E6666 B88 2017 (print) | LCC PS3554.E6666 (ebook)|
DDC 813/54—dc23
LC record available at https://lccn.loc.gov/2016009216

Printed in China
(hc) 10 9 8 7 6 5 4 3 2 1

Illustrations done in watercolor and sumi ink with brush on Saunders Waterford
    watercolor paper
Display type set in Rakugaki by P22
Text type set in Gill Sans by Monotype
Color separations by Colourscan Print Co Pte Ltd Singapore
Printed by 1010 Printing International Limited in Huizhou, Guangdong, China
Production supervision by Brian G. Walker
Designed by Susan Mallory Sherman

Contents

The Night Before

The Secret
Ethan, kindergarten

Before I went to bed,
I put Bear's blue jacket
in the pocket
of my new kindergarten pants.
Grandpa's the only one who knows,
and he promised not to tell.
Bear's jacket is soft and fuzzy
just like him,
and tomorrow,
anytime I want,
I can put my hand in my pocket
and feel it there.

Starting Over
Zach, first grade

Last year I knew everything
about kindergarten.
I knew all the kids
and the teacher.
I knew which was my seat
and how to ask to use the bathroom
and where it was.
Now I have to learn everything
all over again.
What if I make a mistake?

Change of Plans
Katie, second grade

Last week the school sent Mama a letter.
She read it to me,
and it had lots of words, but mostly it said
Miss Kring won't be my teacher
for second grade
like I wanted.
Instead I'll have a new teacher,
someone I don't even know.
The letter said his name is Mr. Patterson.
Teachers at my school aren't called Mr.
Their names begin Miss or Mrs.,
like they're supposed to.
Except for Mr. Liu, but he's for fourth grade,
so that's OK.

Thank You and Please
Jackie, third grade

Sometimes I forget
to say my prayers,
but not tonight.
It wouldn't be good to forget
on the night before third grade.
First I need to say thank you
that we didn't have to move this summer.
Now I can stay at J. W. Riley for another year
and be with kids I know.
Second, I'll say please
don't let Mrs. McKinney be the kind of teacher
who thinks it's a big bother
having me in her room
a whole hour before school starts
so Mama can catch the bus to work.
The Lord listens to every child,
our preacher says.
God must hear a lot of praying
the night before school starts.

What If?
Carlos, fourth grade

Papa comes in to say good night
before he goes to work. He says,
"New school tomorrow—big day, eh?"
"Papa," I say, "I won't know anyone tomorrow.
What if no one likes me?"
Papa laughs.
"Not like? *Un hombre* like you?
So smart, so strong, so handsome?
No es posible."
"It is possible," I argue. "What if—?"
Papa shakes his head.
"So many 'what ifs' from you,
always, always,
and most of them never happen, *verdad*?"
"*Sí*, true," I admit.
He kisses me on the head.
"Tomorrow, when you come home,
you give me names, people who don't like you.
Fifty, one hundred, we fight them all
like *El Vengador,* OK?"
He poses like a fighter,
and we both begin to laugh.

Lights Out
Mia, fifth grade

I shouldn't have to turn off my light this early.
I'm not the least bit sleepy, and
I have everything ready for morning.
My clothes are laid out,
and my supplies are in my book bag:
a three-ring binder and number-two pencils
and some pink erasers that smell like bubble gum.
My school forms are
filled in and signed.
All I have to do in the morning
is decide
if I should put my hair in a ponytail
and let my ears show.
I just wanted to read one more chapter.
Dad should have let me.
After tonight I won't ever have time to read,
because you get lots of homework
in fifth grade.
Everyone says so.
I hope I'm not supposed to have a ruler . . .
or a compass, or a . . .

In the Morning

17

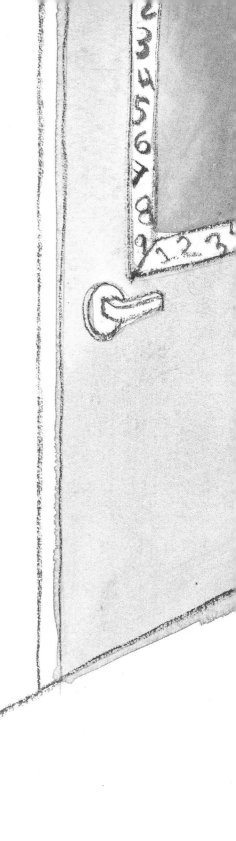

Oh No, the Bell!
Mia, *fifth grade*

I meant to leave sooner,
but I thought I'd read a little
while I ate my cereal.
And then the last chapter was so exciting,
I had to finish.
And I still needed to wash my hands
and put in my hearing aids.
I wanted to get them in just right,
so I was taking my time.
I heard the 7:30 news come on.
I ran down the stairs and grabbed my stuff,
and now I'm running up more stairs
because fifth grade is on the second floor.
The final bell rings
as I get to the room, so
I plop down in the only desk left—
way in back,
right inside the door.
I never sit next to the door,
where the hall sounds get in the way
of what I need to hear.
Tomorrow I'm definitely
leaving earlier.

Feeling Lucky
Carlos, fourth grade

I'm wearing new shoes!
Black with a silver stripe.
They were waiting on the table
with their strings still tied together
when I came into the kitchen.
"A present from your papa!
New school, new shoes. *¡Qué suerte!*" Mama said.
"*Sí*, I'm lucky," I said.
"Lucky to have you and Papa."
I gave her a good-bye hug.
Now I'm swinging my lunch bag round and round
like a pitcher winding up.
I bet I find a new friend quick.
Maybe a kid who likes baseball
and knows who Miguel Cabrera is
will want to eat lunch with me.
I brought an extra bag of chips
just in case.

The Rabbit

Jackie, third grade

A kid named Logan and I
both got here at seven,
and Mrs. McKinney
said she likes having two early birds
to keep her company.
And guess what I found out?
Third grade has a rabbit!
His name is Homer Hoppit.
Last year's third grade named him.
Logan said we should get to choose a new name.
But how can you change anyone's name,
even a rabbit's?
Homer is all gray, except his tummy
is a little bit white,
and inside his ears it's pink.
His nose is always wiggling up and down,
but his mouth chews sideways.
When he moves, his front legs run a little,
then his back legs hop to catch up.
Mrs. McKinney says we can pick him up
when we clean his cage.
I can't wait.

Seven O'Clock Butterflies
Katie, second grade

I think I have a stomachache.
And it wouldn't be smart to start second grade
on a day when I'm feeling sick.
Maybe tomorrow
would be better than today
for starting back to school.
But Mom says, "Your stomach just has butterflies."
And Gram says, "Guess we'd better
call an ambulance."
"That's exactly the way you teased me
  when I was Katie's age,"
  Mom says to Gram.
"You know how angry it made me,
  so why do you do it to Katie?"
  Gram shrugs.
"So butterflies aren't teasing?" she asks.
"Katie doesn't mind.
  She knows what I mean, don't you, honey?"
  I do. What she and Mom both mean is
  they're not going to let me
  stay home today.

A Good Plan
Zach, first grade

J. W. Riley is a big, big school,
but I know the way
to my new room.
I have a map in my head.
I go in the front door
and walk straight down the hall
to the third door.
I know my new teacher's name.
It's Mrs. Wilson.
And I remember what she looks like,
because Miss Knapp took us to meet her
and see her room
at the end of last year.
Mrs. Wilson has very curly hair,
and her voice is a lot louder
than Miss Knapp's.
Everyone says she's nice.
But before I go to my new room,
I think I'll go back to the kindergarten room
and show Miss Knapp
how much taller I am
now that I'm in first grade.

The Crossing Guard
Ethan, kindergarten

Our crossing guard
is Mrs. Tibbs.
She's kind of fat,
and that's good because
the cars can see her really well.
When she walks into the street,
she holds her stop sign high,
and all the cars stop.
But their motors keep going,
rummm, rummm, rummm,
like they can't wait to move.
"You'd think they have someplace
important to go,"
Mrs. Tibbs says,
and then she laughs.
I'm not sure why that's funny,
but I like her laugh,
so I laugh, too.

27

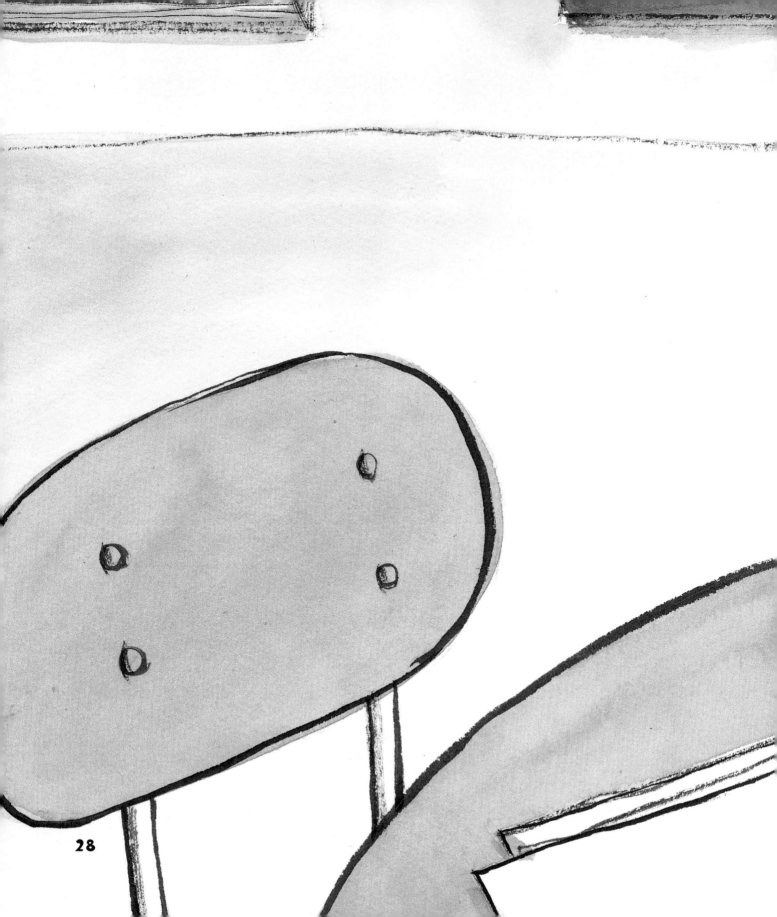

28

At School

Drawing My Family
Ethan, kindergarten

Miss Knapp says the
first day is Get-Acquainted Day
in kindergarten.
Everyone gets a piece of drawing paper
and a box of crayons.
On our paper we are supposed to draw
our family and write their names if we know how.
I draw Mom first, then me holding Bear.
Up in the corner I put
Grandpa in his apartment,
and then I'm finished.
The girl who sits across from me
is named Sophia, and she
draws two brothers and three sisters,
so she takes a long time.
My family looks lonesome on my paper,
so I add a brother and a dog.
That looks better.
Under the brother I write Mike,
and under the dog I write Henry,
but I'm not sure I spelled Henry right.

My New Room
Zach, first grade

In kindergarten we sat at tables,
but this year we have desks.
When I came into the room,
Mrs. Wilson asked,
"Can you find your own desk, Zach?
There's a name on every desk."
I thought I'd found mine near the door,
but that one said Zach G.,
and I'm Zach W.
We didn't have any other Zachs last year.
Maybe Zach G. will be a new friend.
I already have one friend.
His name is Adam.
He was in kindergarten with me,
and now his desk is right behind mine.
Sometimes he leans forward
and whispers in my ear.
It's nice to have an already-friend.

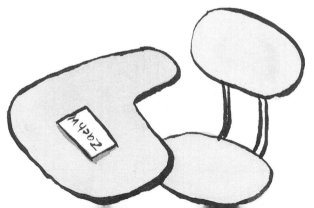

Mistake
Katie, second grade

I made my twos backward.
We were making calendars
for September,
and all my twos were backward.
I didn't know they were
till Melissa told me.
I put my head down on my desk
for a while,
because you can't erase crayon.
Mr. Patterson asked me what was wrong.
And when I told him,
he said, "Never mind—
you'll get them right soon.
I used to make mine backward, too,
and sometimes I still have to think
how they go."
That's funny.
I didn't think teachers
were ever wrong.

Jobs
Jackie, third grade

Third graders can have jobs.
I could be line leader
or the person who changes
the day of the week
on the bulletin board.
I could be plant tender and water the plants
or message runner
and take the lunch count to the office.
But the best job of all—
the one I want—
is feeding Homer Hoppit.
You have to be really responsible
for that.
I didn't get a job for this week,
but maybe next week
when Mrs. McKinney sees
how responsible I am,
I'll be Jackie the rabbit keeper.

Head Count
Carlos, fourth grade

Mr. Liu's taking a head count—
who's buying lunch,
so the cafeteria knows
how many plates of macaroni and cheese
they should be serving up
with green beans and applesauce and two cookies.
I'm taking a head count, too.
So far I've seen only
three guys with brownish skin
and black hair like mine,
and none of them are in my class.
I was thinking I might get lonely,
but then I looked at Mr. Liu again.
He looks like he's OK here,
and I haven't seen anyone
who looks like him.

Mrs. K.
Mia, fifth grade

Mrs. Kysperski is my teacher's name,
but she tells us
we can call her Mrs. K.
I like the way Kysperski sounds,
like someone telling secrets.
Mrs. K. says she doesn't like to be bored,
and she gets bored easily,
so we should get used to having
"Mrs. K.'s Now-and-Then Seat Shuffles."
The first shuffle was right away.
I was one of the people who got shuffled,
and now my desk is up front.
Mrs. K. is like me—she likes poetry.
So first thing every day,
she's going to read us a poem.
I'm lucky I got shuffled, because
now I'll be able
to hear every word she reads!
Fifth grade may be OK after all.
We'll see.

After School

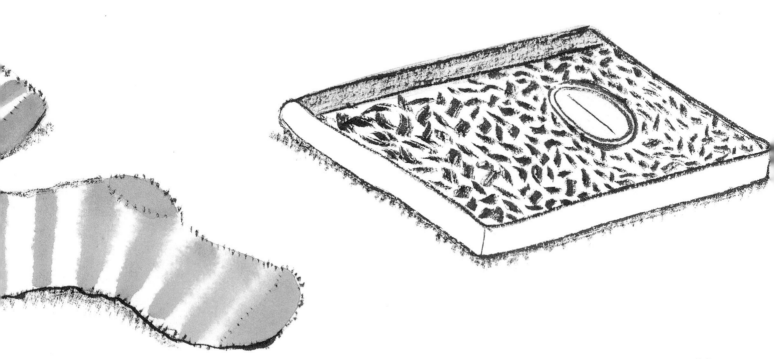

Inspiration
Mia, fifth grade

Dad pokes his head in my room and asks
why I don't have any homework.
I tell him that rearranging my room
is homework,
and so is listening to music while I clean.
Mrs. K. says creative people don't like
to waste time looking for things,
so they keep their tools
(like paintbrushes or pens)
organized and ready to use
when inspiration strikes.
Everyone is creative, she says,
and our job this year
is to discover what inspires
our own creativity
and starts us dreaming.
I wonder what Dad will think
when he sees the poster of
Meg White and her drums
on the wall above my desk.

My List
Carlos, fourth grade

I know how Papa is—
he'll meet me at the door
and right away he'll say,
"*Digame*, tell me,
did any 'what ifs' happen?
How many *malos* need to meet
El Vengador?"
I'll hand him a piece of paper.
"My list," I'll say, looking sad,
and Papa's face will be all serious
when he begins to read what I wrote:
"No bad guys, Papa, no 'what ifs,' but
there's this kid who knows the batting average
of every player on the Tigers' roster.
At recess the two of us played catch,
and we shared my extra chips
on the way home."
Then Papa will smile and ask me,
"What's his name, this new friend of yours?"
And I'll grin and say,
"Her name's Maria."

Checklist
Jackie, third grade

The most important thing in my backpack
is my new silver key chain with my apartment key on it.
The next most important is the little red notebook
where Mama made a list of everything I need to do
every day when I get home from school.
First: bring in the mail. Check.
Second: lock the door behind me. Check.
Third: call Mrs. Blumin in Apartment C, above us,
and let her know I'm home. Check.
Fourth: feed Peek and Boo, my goldfish. Check.
Fifth and sixth: eat my snack and do my homework.
Or, if I don't have any homework,
read or draw until Mama gets home. Check.
This is what I don't do: no matter what, I don't
answer the door, turn on the TV or the stove, or
set off any firecrackers.
"Mama!" I said when she wrote that.
"I wouldn't! You're being foolish."
"Setting off firecrackers stands for foolish," Mama said.
"Keep that in mind." Check.
Tomorrow I'm going to show Mrs. McKinney
my notebook
so she can see the checks
and know how responsible I am.

Mr. Patterson
Katie, second grade

Our class was kind of noisy today,
but Mr. Patterson doesn't mind noise.
This afternoon when I had a question,
he asked me, "Why are you whispering?
Speak up, Quiet Katie!"
I asked a little louder, and he said, "Better, but . . .
show Katie how it's done, Danny Boy."
Then Danny repeated my question.
Danny has the loudest voice in school.
"Think you can beat that, Quiet Katie?"
Mr. Patterson dared me.
So I asked louder, and then Danny did,
and we kept taking turns,
and everybody was laughing
until Mr. Patterson put up his hand.
He said, "Maybe we should be
a wee bit quieter
before we all get in trouble.
Good job, Quiet Katie.
Good job, Danny Boy."
I wonder if I could get Mom and Gram
to take turns getting louder.
Would they start to laugh,
and we could all have fun
together?

Marching Home
Zach, first grade

We're going,
"Hup, two, three, four, hup, two, three,"
like movie soldiers do—
me and Adam and the other Zach.
I never had a friend to walk home with before,
but today I have two!
Adam moved in with his dad,
so now he walks my way,
and Zach G. says his mom will pick him up
anywhere he likes.
At recess this morning we made a plan:
we're going to build a tree house
in an oak tree, like in the story Mrs. Wilson
is reading us.
I can get wood from a woodpile in our basement,
and I've got lots of nails,
so all we have to do is find
an oak tree.
After we have a snack.

Tomorrow
Ethan, kindergarten

I ran and jumped and hopped
all the way to Mrs. Tibbs.
She asked, "How was kindergarten?"
And I said, "It was fun.
I've got twenty-three new friends."
"I guess I'll see you tomorrow, then," she said,
and laughed.
I guess she likes to laugh.
Tomorrow I think I'll leave Bear's jacket
at home. I'll bet he got cold without it.
Tomorrow I think
I'll tell Miss Knapp that
I don't really have a brother named Mike
or a dog named Henry,
and she'll probably say
sometimes she wishes she had a dog.
Kindergarten's not as hard
as I thought it would be.